T0355846

Also by r.h. Sin

Whiskey Words & a Shovel

Whiskey Words & a Shovel II

Whiskey Words & a Shovel III

Rest in the Mourning

A Beautiful Composition of Broken

Algedonic

Planting Gardens in Graves

Planting Gardens in Graves Volume Two

Planting Gardens in Graves Volume Three

She Felt Like Feeling Nothing

Empty Bottles Full of Stories

She Just Wants to Forget

Falling Toward the Moon

We Hope This Reaches You in Time

A Crowded Loneliness

She's Strong, but She's Tired

She Fits Inside These Words

Winter Roses after Fall

Dream, My Child

Anywho, I Love You

I Hope She Finds This

I Hope This Reaches Her in Time Revised Edition

Come Back to Me

This Day Is Dark

Beautiful Sad Eyes, Weary Waiting for Love

Ascending Assertion

A Midnight Moon

The Year of Letting Go: 365 Days Pursuing Emotional Freedom

NEW MOONS

NEW MOONS
PHASES OF HEALING

r.h. Sin

Andrews McMeel
PUBLISHING®

CONTENTS

o

INTRODUCTION

Through therapy, I discovered that I've never been in a relationship that wasn't rooted in disappointment and toxicity. This realization has been the most heartbreaking thing to come to grips with. This belief that I have never known a love that would last, nor what it means to be with someone who would hold me at the center of their actions and decisions for all time, was something that tore through my heart with ease. When you talk out these things with an objective party, you come to the understanding not only that you don't know what it means to be loved unconditionally but also that you're the one deciding to end up in spaces that aren't entirely healthy for you.

I think sitting with that for days on end pushed me to a sort of mental break. I was in the deepest depression I'd ever known, and the hardest part was that I felt like I couldn't even speak about it. Do you know what that feels like? Do you know what feeling like that makes you think you want to do? My life has been a constant story of heartbreak and depression. So much of this began in my childhood, which truly affected my adult life is a miserable way. It's funny—or not—that when I look back on my catalog of writing, I realize I've been screaming at myself from the pages, unknowingly admitting to my sadness and sharing that energy with those of you who could relate to those feelings. And so, this is why, of all people, I'd like to take your hand and waltz into a more beautiful space.

Over time, something began to happen. Something I never saw coming. I woke up one morning to feel that everything that had been sitting heavily on my chest and inside my soul was gone. There was this deep and beautiful feeling of relief. I'm trying my best to describe it, but when I woke up that day, it was like I'd become a different person. To this day, I sometimes believe that I jumped timelines, somehow ending up in a reality completely opposite of the one in which I was living. Whatever it was, whatever had happened as my body entered a deep state of sleep, I emerged from it with a bliss, a clear awakening, and a newfound belief in my life.

This is when my story fully took on elements of healing. This is when my narrative transformed tremendously, and I guess I just want to give that gift to you. My hope is that, as you read this, your heart begins to feel new life and your mind begins to process all that has hurt you up to this moment. Or maybe you're far along in your journey and just need a perspective shift that will help you sustain where you are and move you along a path that will lead to greater heights in your emotional development.

REFLECTIONS

I WANT TO KNOW YOU AND YOUR TRAGIC STORY OF LOVE. I WANT TO LISTEN AS YOU SPEAK OF THE LOWS THAT HAVE INSPIRED THIS HIGH DESIRE FOR SOMETHING SPECIAL. I WANT TO KNOW YOU AND YOUR PAIN; I WANT TO UNDERSTAND HOW YOU WERE ABLE TO REMAIN RELENTLESS IN YOUR NATURE, STRONG-WILLED IN THE FACE OF EVERYTHING MEANT TO DESTROY YOU. I WANT TO LEARN FROM YOUR AWAKENING, KNOW YOUR WAYS, AND KNOW WHAT YOU DID TO CULTIVATE A BEAUTIFUL CLARITY. TEACH ME HOW TO BE MORE LIKE THE WARRIOR THAT LIVES IN YOUR SOUL; SHOW ME YOUR TRUTH SO THAT I CAN REMEMBER WHAT IT TAKES TO GET THROUGH THE FIRE. AND AS YOU READ THESE WORDS, YOU DISCOVER THAT IT IS ME LEANING ON YOU FOR A GREATER UNDERSTANDING.

o

I have always viewed the moon as a source of healing energy. I found that when the days weighed me down, when I'd be forced to sit with my feelings as the sun hid itself, the moon became a sort of counsel, a friend, a loved one. I think back on my life and how the natural elements in our existence have always been more reliable and consistent than even the people who have claimed to love us and how, without fail, the moon has always shown up to sit with me in the depths of darkness, unwavering and ready to cast its light upon me. And maybe you feel that way as well. Maybe you've never even considered them until now, the healing properties of a night sky draped in the light of an imperfect but beautiful moon.

o

I promise you that if you took the time to know her heart, you'd discover a love that has no limits. If you understood her mind, I promise you'd give in to that urge to acknowledge her brilliance. To know her soul is to see magic; to be in her presence is to experience a richness in spirit. She's rare, one of a kind, because she's authentically herself. She's strong not because she's never fallen but because she's been able to pick herself back up and push forward even when she felt she couldn't go on. There have been many obstacles placed in front of her body—mountains with peaks that scrape the clouds and fire dancing broadly on the path where she's meant to walk—and still, nothing has been able to slow her down.

She sees challenges as a gift; she transmutes pain into power and wisdom. Warrior blood flows in her veins, a mystic's perspective resides in her mind, and the heart of a goddess beats in her chest. Her eyes move left to right. At this moment, I've come to realize the true power in her presence as she holds this book in her hands. She is you as you go through phases of evolution. Finding your light in the breath of darkness. Rediscovering all that you are and all that you will be in this new era of healing and peace.

o

Something beautiful is about to emerge and enter your life. I want you to know that the more you choose yourself and lean into the things that help to calm your nervous system, the more you prioritize your peace of mind and mental health, the closer you are to a love life that will not break you down or call on you to compromise the peace you've cultivated in this season of your life.

o

There is this beautiful idea that I've always held on to, especially at the end of any relationship I initially thought would last: no matter what, if you lead with love, and if the love you gave to another person is truly genuine, then in the event of that relationship ending, it just means that the person you chose is choosing to get out of the way, so as to allow you the chance to be with the one you're meant to be with.

When people hurt you, overlook you, fail to appreciate you, and lie to or betray you, they are simply telling you that you deserve something they are not capable of providing. And while you sometimes want to cling to that person regardless of the pain they've caused, you have to accept the fact that the love of your life and the person you're meant to be with is still out there somewhere.

Please be patient with and kind to yourself as you learn to navigate loss, heartbreak, and the trauma that follows. I write this from a place of love and admiration for the way you show up every day in this life, ready to reclaim all that is meant for you.

O

Look at you, beloved, a woman emerging from the fire, a phoenix. You were transformed by the things that were meant to destroy you. I not only fall in love with this idea of you rising from ashes, more beautiful and wiser than ever, but that love lives beneath the surface. It is focused on the seed in tainted soil from which you grew roots. Your soul is plastered in magic, your heart is made of gold, and yet you've had to face heartbreak and disappointment time and time again. You've struggled a bit, stumbled a bit, then reset to reestablish your seated position on a throne in front of the kingdom you built on your own.

I write this to celebrate your existence; I write this to acknowledge the facts. No matter the trouble, no matter the circumstance. You figure out what moves to make, what direction to go, and what actions to take. Inside you lives a pack of wolves—no, a load of lightning—no, a universe filled with endless possibilities, and in all that, in all that you are, there is a heart made for love, deserving of magic. Inside you there is a future that aligns with a divine purpose.

Damn, you know what . . . I guess I wrote all this to say that I love who you are, and I love what you are becoming. Let nothing dim your shine, beloved.

Your favorite writer,
SIN

o

It takes entirely too long to understand that the things you want in a partner are not based on a myth or some unrealistic dream. You don't even realize it in the beginning, but what you desire becomes nearly impossible because of your choices in a mate. You see, even with the best intentions, you decide to be with someone who speaks to the all-too-familiar pain that lives within your heart. You choose partners who mirror the trauma, unknowingly setting yourself up for a lack of belief in everything your heart requires to feel loved.

You go through so much shit that you arrive at this notion that everything you now want out of your relationship doesn't exist. Even your past partners mirror that. Your ex, horrible as they were to you, will tell you that there is nothing better out there, and the fear of being alone will almost push you back toward a relationship that was never worthy of your energy.

o

Perfection doesn't exist, but there is someone you won't have to force into spaces in your life. There is someone who doesn't want to keep you hidden. There is someone who will appreciate your kindness and match the energy you give. There is someone who won't tell you lies and won't betray you. There is someone willing to do the work. Someone who will be willing to grow beside you.

Eventually, you realize that the quest for the perfect partner isn't about chasing a nonexistent ideal but rather about finding someone who complements the reality of who you are. This person understands and respects your journey, acknowledges your past, and sees the beauty in your scars. They don't seek to fix you but to walk with you, offering a hand when you stumble and a smile to celebrate your triumphs. They're not a mirror of your traumas but a beacon of hope for your healing, showing you that love, in its true form, is not about perfection but about acceptance, growth, and a willingness to see the light even in the darkest moments. With them, you learn that love is real, attainable, and worth every step of the journey, no matter how long it takes to find.

o

you want revenge at first
you feel jaded, disappointed
and hurt
you want revenge at first
but then you begin to realize
that all the lies
were just setting you free
you realize that the heartache
was just giving you
a better reason to leave
you want revenge at first
but there's nothing worse
than wasting your emotional output
on someone who no longer deserves
an emotional reaction
so, you move on
you gain traction
you heal, and that healing
causes a chain reaction

for better things to happen
giving life to a more beautiful attraction
and one day, you'll look back on everything
you'll smile and maybe start laughing
hindsight says you'll get through it
you'll get past them
and you'll be their biggest regret
whenever other people ask them
You want revenge at first
but to a degree
the revenge is that they lose
and you gain the most important of keys
the ability to unlock a door
that leads you to the relationship
in which you're meant to be

o

I HAVE TO GET OUT OF THIS PLACE; IT'S LIKE
EVERY TIME I FEEL AN OUNCE OF PEACE, IT IS
STRIPPED AWAY AND PUSHED FURTHER BACK
TO THOSE UNHEALED MOMENTS, TRIGGERED
BY THE SAME WORDS MY MOTHER USED TO
BELITTLE WHATEVER PROGRESS I MADE, AND
IT'S ALWAYS THE SAME THING. PEOPLE DON'T
ACKNOWLEDGE YOUR CHANGES. THE ONES WHO
ARE BROKEN OR STUCK IN THEIR WAYS REFUSE
TO SEE HOW HARD YOU WORK, HOW MUCH YOU
DO, OR HOW OFTEN YOU CONTRIBUTE, EVEN TO
THEIR OWN LIVES. AND SO THEY IGNORE ALL
THE GOOD THAT EXISTS IN YOU UNTIL THEY
FIND A WEAK SPOT THAT HOLDS EITHER ALL
THOSE SUPPRESSED FEELINGS OR WHATEVER
REMNANTS ARE LEFT FROM BEFORE, AND YOU
FIND YOURSELF BACK IN THAT SAME PIT, THE
PIT YOU WISH TO ESCAPE FROM. THE PIT
YOUR PARENTS PLACED YOU IN WITH THEIR
MISTREATMENT AND NEGLECT. YOU'VE LIVED
THERE SO LONG, AND YOU'VE HAD TO TIRELESSLY
NAVIGATE THOSE SPACES WITHOUT ANY HELP . . .

O

You will miss me when your worth is overlooked.

You will miss me when no one you meet talks you into their future.

You will miss me when you begin to consider shrinking yourself for a relationship out of loneliness.

You will miss all the nights we could have had, all the laughs we could have had.

You will miss my consideration when the people you choose have no concern about how you feel.

You will miss being seen as something more than your assets.

You will miss having your dreams supported.

You will miss the way my presence in your life nurtured progression, peace, and enlightenment.

You will miss being loved throughout all your changes.

You will miss not being pressured into things with which you're not comfortable.

You will miss the way I decided to pour into you even when I was empty with nothing left, and how the thought of it being my last breath didn't scare me because I was willing to give that to you.

You will miss these arms; they guided you.

You will miss this calm, the way it made you feel safe.

o

time wasted on a lie that felt like the truth
energy invested into giving my all to you
years of support in an instant forgotten
fresh fruit and roses
now wilted and rotten
for the nights I felt broken
tears soaked through the cotton
kept going with no concern
and no intention of stoppin'
dependable, useful
I knew the mission
did the job
but when I need it
I don't see you
and I think that's kinda odd
so of course
I should be angry
I should be yelling through the roof
never hold yourself accountable
and it's me that you will lose

you talk big right now
see, you don't care right now
but in time, it'll hit you
when the lights go down
you'll return to where I met you
confused, cold, and lonely
and I take pleasure in knowing
that when I'm gone, you'll never know me

O

"I hate you" is what I felt
but the truth is
I hate the fact
that you make the same choices
as someone who hates themselves
I'm tired, somewhat broken
weary-hearted, feeling robbed
I guess it's true; you hurt others
when you self-sabotage

o

You THOUGHT IT WAS A LOSS, BUT IN THE ABSENCE OF THE PERSON WHO REFUSED TO CARE FOR YOU PROPERLY, YOU DISCOVERED THAT YOU COULD BE THE SOURCE OF YOUR OWN HAPPINESS AND PEACE.

○

It's so wild when you think about how much time can go into trying to foster a relationship with the person you're not meant to be with. You trick yourself into believing that, because relationships aren't perfect, the things you experience when you're with someone are somehow normal and necessary, and yet, when you finally begin to heal, you come to realize that relationships are that difficult only when you're with the wrong person.

Yes, perfection doesn't exist, but there is a relationship into which you will fit perfectly. There is a relationship that won't call upon your heart to ache or your mind to be plagued with confusion. There is a relationship that will help you along your path of inner peace and personal growth. There is a relationship that will encourage you in all the ways you've always dreamed. And the moment you refuse to settle for a love that hurts you is when you can begin to establish room and space for a healthier, more genuine version of love.

o

THIS SADNESS IS JUST A CHAPTER; IT'S
NOT THE ENTIRE STORY OF YOUR LIFE.

o

You're reading this, aren't you? Heart heavy, full of things you want to give and share, but you've yet to find someone worthy of the profound and beautiful experience of being with you. And so, sometimes you read my writing and start to dream of a love that'll last, like the love I often find myself writing about. Here, at this moment, is a safe place to feel all your feelings without the fear of being overlooked or taken for granted.

There is a loneliness you've felt, and it's not like you've been single this entire time—hell, maybe you're with someone right now—yet the feelings of loneliness sit in your chest. You come here because you know I'm speaking to you directly. You know, deep down, that you inspire all the things in my heart. It's like I tune in to the channel that serves only your energy, and I willingly allow you to speak through me. I just want to say this while I have your attention: you are meant for the most beautiful love with someone who will cherish you for what feels like an eternity, and even though you look over at the time with the thought that maybe your luck has run out, I just want you to always remember that it isn't too late for you. As long as you're willing to heal and preserve your energy, the right thing will enter your life, and you will no longer relate to what is written here. Even if that means I lose you, I'd rather see you happy and in love.

o

D on't stay because of age.
Don't stay out of fear of loneliness.

Don't stay because of the time invested.

Don't stay because you're afraid that they'll treat the next person better.

And never stay for the kids.

Life is too short to settle for something that doesn't mirror the type of love your heart requires.

o

You're in a season of leaving things behind. And it's not easy, but you've come to understand that in order to make room for peace and joy, you must first let go of those who no longer align with the way you envision your life.

o

A t a very early age, I came to the realization that calmness in my spirit is the most important feeling to me. I realized the very first time I felt it that I would do anything and give up everything just to maintain that feeling. I can still recall the moment in 2001—it was a Sunday. I wasn't feeling well, so I wasn't able to tag along to church with my family. I was left behind, and little did I know that, in those moments, I would experience something I never knew I truly needed, something profound and unknown to me. There was a powerful silence in the air, an absence of tension. Voices that often yelled became muted, and my anxiety disappeared. That's when I knew what had to happen. That was the moment when I identified peace as the single most important thing to me.

For about three hours, I sat up in my bed, seemingly drifting into this zone of solace. The quiet allowed me an opportunity to look inward. It was something I didn't have a word for at the time, but nonetheless, the experience was life-changing. In the three hours that passed, I went on a sort of trip, and the wild part is, that's when I knew I would be here in this moment, telling this to you. That was the day I realized I wanted to write professionally.

When my family returned, the dream ended, and I was tossed back into a narcissistic storm of abuse and distress.

Sometimes you have to lose something for a moment in order to fully understand that its absence is a gift.

Say that out loud, repeat it, keep it, and remember that last sentence. It's important. It's something I wrote years ago. It's something I say to myself each and every day.

I feel as though, after that moment, the foundation for me was laid, and my fantasy of peace ran rampant all throughout my head. Of course, due to my lack of understanding of how trauma affects a person, I would seemingly find myself in environments where my peace was deliberately shaken or stripped away from me for a variety of reasons and justifications, but in the back of my head, I knew peace would always be my ultimate goal.

There is nothing more important than peace of mind. The calm you feel enables you to be open to healthy relationships. It fosters closeness between you and the people who appreciate your presence.

I know that in this life, it's so easy to be codependent on others, and sadly, so many of us understand what it means to try and lean on the very things and people who ruin our nervous systems, but discovering the courage to walk away is the most powerful skill you can ever harness.

Do not sit and rest in pits surrounded by tension and unnecessary drama. Do not lay your head down beside people who mistreat you or fail to value your presence in their lives. Move until you find a safe place to sit. Walk away until you find a moment of solace. Move away until you find a home that has a positive foundation, one that amplifies whatever joy you've cultivated on your own.

Time and time again, I lean on the understanding that a beautiful life can be acquired only when you make beautiful choices, and decisions rooted in a desire for peace are the most beautiful of all.

This is our era to choose peace over everything so that we can be everything to ourselves and to those who rely on us.

o

Consider for a moment all in your life that causes you to feel things that do not align with the experience you desire. You wake up each day, and as you interact with your surroundings, you discover that there are things in your ecosystem that fill you with emotions that are not helpful in your journey toward cultivating a healthy and meaningful life.

Today, maybe even now, I'd like you to take five minutes for yourself and make either a physical or a mental list of everything that makes your life feel less than what you dream it to be. I want you to think of the cause and effect of what you give your time to.

Maybe you feel a sense of peace in the absence of a particular person. Maybe you are overwhelmed with anxiety whenever a particular name passes into your mind. Pay attention to those feelings of loneliness that weigh you down when in the presence of a certain someone or even a group of people.

o

Today, I open my arms to receive all the good things that may have been hidden behind the pain I've felt. I am no longer willing to remain a prisoner stuck behind bars made to obstruct and distract me from experiencing the life and love I deserve.

I set free the urge to hold on to people and things that do not align with the person I am becoming and the life I'm choosing to lead.

I understand that I harness the power to free myself from the weight of someone's negativity or inability to regulate themselves emotionally. I am not obligated to make room for people who intend to tear me down or hold me back.

I set myself free from the burden of pleasing people.

There is peace in letting go.

There is self-love in saying no.

There is freedom in choosing myself.

Today, I open my heart to experience all the peace that life has to offer me in the big and small moments.

o

To the most brilliant woman reading this: I want you to go where the love flows freely. I want you to go where the love feels safe. Where the love inspires you to grow and bloom. To the queen reading these words: I hope you never give up on that dream of love you have in your heart. To the woman staring at this page, reading these words: Thank you for the gift of your presence. Thank you for giving me your time and for inspiring me with your light. I hope you feel love when you read this. I hope you feel seen when you see this.

O

I've been moving from a place of love and being kind to myself, even on my worst days. The sight of dark clouds used to make me feel anxious, but now I've come to see them as an opportunity to learn how to dance in the rain. I see beauty in the void; that emptiness just looks like a place set aside for me and a soulmate. I see a fire and don't think about how it would feel to get burned; I see the flames as warmth for a weary traveler.

You see, my perspective has changed so much that there are times when I don't even recognize the person looking back at me, and that alone has inspired me to continue to be more than I'd ever hoped. I've been laughing in the faces of those who thought I'd come up short or belittle myself to fit where they are. I know it hurts them to see that their triggers no longer work, and the only trigger left is the one they've pulled upon themselves.

I love it here, a place of endless beauty, a moment of love in abundance. I used to dream of this. I'd wander so long that daytime bled into night until I was lost, but I found it here. The present, the place where all I could ever want exists. I just had to stop looking in the wrong direction or to the wrong people for what they were incapable of providing.

And I want you to know this, too; I want you to find what I've found. I want you to understand that there are people in the world so broken, they do not desire healing; they give in to the urge to bring others down. They tell lies to make themselves feel better, and they will trigger you into reactions just to justify their bad intentions. The only way to win is to not play their game. The only way to get to the point of true peace is to refrain from any engagement with them. The only way to live the life you dream is to abandon the notion that you must fight for people who have decided they will never fight for themselves.

It's time to free yourself . . . It's time to live again. It's time to welcome a midnight moon for its renewing and healing purposes.

O

I've been nurturing myself, refusing to compromise my light, integrity, or self-respect. Bonding with others with whom I share this path of self-love. Spending more of my energy on the things that encourage fulfillment and joy. I let peace wash over me, cultivating more as I learn how to best navigate through my days or any struggles that may enter my point of view.

It's getting easier. The more I practice, the greater my self-reliance, the more profound my reflection as I look to myself for what I need, knowing that, ultimately, I am the source of all I've ever wanted.

I know my children see and feel the change in me. This is evident by those random tiny kisses they give me throughout the day, as if to say, *Thank you for giving us your best.* Or the way my closest friends reach for me with messages that feel like tight hugs or the clasping of two hands, interlocking to express a deep connection. This part of my life is truly a blessing. Not to say the moments before this weren't, but in my mindfulness and intentionality, I can truly see the gifts in the present. I understand more and more how my decisions shape the rest of my days and the relationships I have to maintain.

And you can do this, too. You can live the way you wish, protected against those who would prefer to dictate your mood or your future results. All you have to remember is that you alone can sculpt your reality into whatever you wish. Want love, be love, and give it to yourself. If you want kindness, be kind and give it to yourself.

I'm blessed to have reached a point in my life where I'm out of reach of the influence of people struggling so much in this life that they choose to hurt and bring others down.

It's time to take back your life.

○

This morning, after some breathwork, I had a moment of clarity. I mean a literal moment of clarity in which you were revealed to me. I mean, it's happened before, but never so clearly. I like to think that I can feel you, so seeing you in my mind's eye is a beautiful thing to witness.

You're not always up-front with some of the stress you've been feeling lately, and it's not because you wish to lie about it; there are just certain things you keep to yourself. But you can't really keep it from me, because I SEE YOU and I feel you as you read this right now.

Life isn't easy; there are moments in the day that will cause you to feel anxious. There are even people in your life who seem to be strategically placed in certain spots to either push your buttons or serve as a distraction to all the things you need and deserve, but these people are lessons. They can also serve as reminders of your strength, and yeah, I get it, you don't always want to be strong, but maybe you don't have to. Maybe, right now, you just be YOU, FEEL WHAT YOU FEEL, and maybe smile a little with the understanding that you're on my mind.

No matter where you are or what you feel, you are important. You are special. You deserve genuine love and understanding. You are supported and considered. YOU ARE YOU, and in every moment of this life, especially this day, YOU ARE ENOUGH.

○

I reflect on the years I spent getting upset with people who were either intentional in their actions or lacked the self-awareness to do better. These actions end up in a box filled with everything you can't control. That box is also filled with everything that doesn't necessarily require an emotional response, but it took me so many years to realize this.

When you practice a quiet acceptance of others and their behaviors, you silently and calmly decide for yourself that they are no longer worthy of your energy, your words, or your time. Reaching this mindset increases the overall peace in your life and creates more room for joy. It is much easier to calmly look at what someone does and say, "Okay," and move on once you understand that they can neither change nor wish to, and none of that is your business. Their actions have nothing to do with you. They are just being who they are, and, armed with that information, you get to choose what you'd like to do.

I'm in the season of letting go of what no longer serves me nor enriches my path, and I think you're there with me, trying to figure out which way to go. And so, today, I want you to practice QUIET ACCEPTANCE and watch how worthless your life becomes in the face of those who mean you emotional harm and distress.

o

Remember to become an observer to any thought that seems to compromise your peace of mind. Imagine yourself in a vehicle passing by, slowing to observe but moving forward.

o

You'll never be a safe place for someone
who prefers to self-sabotage.

o

Passing in and out of a woman's life is not a flex. Securing her devotion and love by matching her energy for what could be a lifetime is.

o

IT'S WILD BECAUSE YOUR PARTNER WANTS
YOU TO PRACTICE SELF-CONTROL WHENEVER
YOUR ANGER IS CAUSED BY THEIR LACK
OF SELF-CONTROL WHEN CHOOSING TO
DO THINGS THAT TRIGGER YOU.

O

Know the difference between loving someone the way you want to love them and loving someone the way they need you to love them.

o

THAT THIRD LOVE IS THE ONE.

o

Heal your past trauma so that you
can both love properly and accept
the healthiest version of love.

o

You CAN PRACTICE ACCEPTING SOMEONE
FOR WHO THEY ARE AND, AT THE SAME TIME,
REMOVE THEM FROM YOUR LIFE IF THEIR
CHARACTER COMPROMISES YOUR PEACE.

O

You tried to hurt me, but in truth
you were setting me free because
you didn't think you deserved my
love, and you were right.

Thank you.

o

HERE I WAS, AFRAID TO GET BURNED . . .
THINKING THE FIRE WOULD HARM ME, BUT ALL
THIS TIME, THE FLAMES WERE A FRIEND, AND
THEIR TOUCH HELPED FORGE A STRONGER ME.

o

IT'S WILD BECAUSE YOU EXPECT THE
BEST VERSION OF ME BUT WANT ME TO
SETTLE FOR YOU AT YOUR WORST.

o

THERE ARE THESE MOMENTS WHEN YOUR EYES MEET YOUR REFLECTION. MOMENTS WHEN THE PALMS OF YOUR HANDS REST SOFTLY ON YOUR SKIN. YOUR TOP AND BOTTOM LIPS MEET LIKE A KISS. UNDERSTAND THAT THOSE MOMENTS ARE A WAY FOR YOU TO RETURN TO YOURSELF. IT IS A RETURN TO HOME. IT IS A RETURN TO PEACE. A RETURN TO MAGIC.

o

WHEN YOU START HEALING, YOU BEGIN
TO REALIZE THAT YOU'VE BEEN CHOOSING
PARTNERS FROM A PLACE IN YOUR HEART
THAT HAS FELT BROKEN FOR FAR TOO LONG.

o

The only way to put an end to a cycle of choosing the wrong person to be with is to focus on healing the parts of your heart that have been traumatized by those who couldn't love you in the way you needed.

It took me too long to realize that I'd been choosing a mate from a place of unprocessed trauma. The moment you realize this is the moment you understand why your relationships are all typically the same.

Turn your energy inward. Begin to focus on healing. Define the love you need and require by giving it to yourself first. This is how you manifest a proper relationship.

o

The more I heal, the more
I need to let go of you.

○

I LOST YOU, AND THINGS GOT BETTER.
I LOST YOU AND GAINED ALIGNMENT.

o

THE ONLY THING AN EX CAN DO FOR ME IS
SHOW ME WHAT TO AVOID MOVING FORWARD.

O

You never need to chase a man. When he genuinely wants you, he's either running in your direction or walking beside you.

o

CONVERSATIONS FLOW EASILY WHEN
YOU'RE TALKING TO THE RIGHT PERSON.

COMMUNICATION IS MATCHED.
NO CONFUSION, JUST TRANSPARENCY.

NEVER IGNORE THAT ABILITY TO BE OPEN.

THAT SHIT IS SO RARE NOWADAYS.

o

WHAT'S COMING IS BETTER
THAN WHAT HURT YOU.

O

You don't have to be perfect. I just want someone who is making an effort to heal. That's the most attractive thing to me.

o

WHAT I'M SEARCHING FOR HAS
BEEN SEARCHING FOR ME.

O

GIVE ME A CALM LOVE. MY MAIN
DESIRE IS PEACE. LET'S MOVE IN
HARMONY. LET'S FALL WITH EASE.

o

I'M NOT SAYING THE GRASS IS ALWAYS
GREENER, BUT I WILL SAY THAT SOMETIMES
YOU HAVE TO STOP WATERING THE
GARDEN BY YOURSELF. IT TAKES TWO.

o

When you begin to heal your trauma,
you look back at your exes like "What
the fuck was I even thinking?"

o

There's an awakening happening. You feel it each morning whenever you open your eyes. There's this overwhelming sense of hope despite the realization that you're waking up in a place you no longer wish to be. Your movements begin to feel different. There's a change in the way you speak, both to others and internally. This slow evolution is so profound in your character that the people around you are beginning to see how different you're becoming. And while there are people who cheer you on and support this change—it's evident in the way they compliment you—there are those in your space that seem to be threatened by this newfound light in your eyes. The proof of this lives in the way they attempt to demean you or criticize the way you are, afraid of what you'll become in the absence of their negativity and disapproval. But despite those comments, you continue forward in pursuit of everything that's been kept from you. You continue on a path filled with obstacles, even paving new ways of travel not just for yourself but for those who may follow after you've found your way.

Isn't it beautiful, the path you walk? The determination in your heart despite the times it's been broken? The way you've put yourself back together is so masterful that it would appear to others like you were never broken in the first place.

o

One thought I'm always plagued by is my inability to find not only a relationship that lasts but one in which love doesn't feel like a fading transaction or like it was built upon surface-level conditions. While I continue to grow in my thinking of what love is, I'm fully understanding and accepting that, with my track record, I definitely know what it isn't.

Part of the reason why we fall into a love that isn't meant to last is this need to fill the void of not knowing what it genuinely means to be loved in a healthy manner.

I'm a bit of a romantic, and while the love I dream up isn't perfect, it at least allows my heart to smile, or at the very least, it doesn't fill my mind with regret.

In the past, I'd let bits of resentment build up, so much so that I'd be filled with rage or sadness or both. And after every transgression or action that made me feel overlooked or unappreciated, I'd argue, trade negative energy, and eventually apologize for the way I handled it, but, looking back, often I'd been owning up to what I'd done while nearly excusing the things that upset or hurt me in the first place. When I reflect on my past relationships, I see plenty of reasons to run the other way, plenty of reasons to take the exit. We get fed these lines about how relationships aren't perfect or how people aren't perfect, and as they embed themselves into our subconscious, we look at every action as a mistake or a symptom of being human when most of those things are always reasons to move on.

I'm also a classic fixer because of the way my childhood was set up …

Plagued by this idea that I can fix a person who isn't even aware of what's broken or doesn't even care.

I can say that my preferences have been changed by everything I've gone through. I have a better understanding of what won't work, so maybe that will put me on a path to discovering something that will.

Maybe the more you heal, the more likely you are to find yourself in new relationships that will not require more healing.

Maybe the more you better yourself, the easier it is to attract relationships that free up more energy for self-love and self-improvement.

As I write this, I'm overwhelmed by the thought that it was my own brokenness that made me feel content in relationships deemed toxic. And how my unresolved childhood issues have caused me to choose relationships that mirror that trauma.

o

Focus on healing more than you focus on pursuing a relationship.

In general, I've learned that by working on myself, reducing moments of anger or resentment, and improving my pathway toward peace. My life has opened up in the way of creating magnetism to things and people who inspire the right types of feelings by supporting my desire to experience positivity and joy. And while you shouldn't rely on people to make you happy, it helps to know people who are on that same journey in healing, people who value the good things that can be hidden in everyday life.

Think of love as a skyscraper. You should be focused on building it through self-love and enlightenment of the heart and soul. The more you focus on that, the stronger that skyscraper can be, and its vastness can eventually be shared with the right person.

Healing is how you avoid the wrong people, the wrong circumstances, and the wrong relationships. Healing is how you protect and preserve your future. Healing is how you detach from what keeps you feeling stuck in cycles of misguided anger, resentment, and sadness.

Healing is love itself, and it's been the greatest romance I've ever known.

o

You may be in a rush for love, but when you look back, you'll realize how often you wasted energy in relationships that weren't built to last. And all that love you gave should've been invested in yourself and healing the wounds you picked up along the way. But I guess the heartbreak serves its purpose because, personally, I'm here, trying to be a better me so that I never have to experience all the bullshit I've gone through in my pursuit of love.

o

The wrong relationship is a prison. You struggle to get yourself free, but the longer you stay, the harder it becomes to see the exit. I want you to understand that while the road ahead can be tough, you've proven to be stronger than you realize. I want you to remember that you are fully capable of doing what is necessary to give life to your future.

o

TO BE SOMEONE'S LAST LOVE AFTER YOU'VE
SPENT THE MAJORITY OF YOUR LIFE IN THE
WRONG RELATIONSHIPS IS A BEAUTIFUL DREAM.

O

I DON'T WANT TO DISTRACT YOU AS YOU
HEAL, AND I KNOW YOU HAVE THE ABILITY
TO DO YOU WHILE ENTERTAINING SOMEONE
NEW, BUT I JUST WANT TO GIVE YOU ROOM
TO LOVE ON YOURSELF COMPLETELY. YOU'VE
GIVEN SO MUCH TO THOSE WHO WERE
UNWORTHY, AND I JUST WANT TO WITNESS
YOU GIVE IT ALL TO YOURSELF FOR A BIT.

o

TRUST ME WHEN I SAY—OVER THIRTY, HEALING
AND WORKING THROUGH YOUR TRAUMA,
BREAKING GENERATIONAL CURSES—THE
LOVE THAT COMES WHILE YOU'RE WORKING
ON YOURSELF WILL BE THE HEALTHIEST
LOVE YOU'LL HAVE EVER EXPERIENCED.

o

Sometimes you have to lose a thing
for a moment to fully understand
that the absence of it is a gift.

O

alignment in love
alignment in peace
alignment in all things

o

That narcissist will not keep you
from the love you deserve.

o

SELF-CARE IS A LOVE STORY YOU'VE
WRITTEN ON YOUR OWN.

O

I wish you a softer love, a
romance full of depth.

o

IT'S SIMPLE: I'M NOT MAKING ANY
ROOM IN MY LIFE FOR PEOPLE WHO
DISRUPT MY NERVOUS SYSTEM.

o

There is a symphony in my heart being composed only for you. A song inspired by not only your existence but also your awakening as you continue this journey of healing and processing the trauma you've experienced in your past. The melody that you are helping me create is something rare and full of depth. The melody that you are helping me create is the most beautiful song that anyone will ever hear, and it is only when we meet each other at the center of love that this composition can be completed. I know you're tired, and I am also, but we have only a bit longer to go before we discover true love on the lines in the notes.

o

No longer am I inspired by the loves I've lost. My hands grew tired of writing about the same old things, cycles that I created from my unwillingness to heal. No longer am I inspired by pain that I didn't deserve or a lie that sounded like the truth when it was first told. I am moving from a place of genuine love, and so genuine love is the only thing that can move me.

o

It's okay. You will find the
purpose in this pain you feel.

o

YOUR SCARS ARE POEMS, SMALL STORIES OF A
GREAT JOURNEY AND A PROFOUND VICTORY.

O

Despite being shattered, you
found a way to rise.

o

THE WOUNDS WILL HEAL, AND WHAT WILL BE
LEFT BEHIND ARE STRENGTH AND WISDOM.

o

Be fierce in your love for self.

o

FEELING BROKEN IS NOT THE SAME AS BEING
DEFEATED. I KNOW IT HURTS, BUT DON'T
LET THEM STOP YOU FROM FIGURING OUT
A WAY TO GET THEM OUT OF YOUR LIFE.

o

You've been growing through this even when it has felt like you're stuck, incapable of moving. Be gentle with yourself as you flow into the understanding of everything you're meant to know, slowly becoming everything you're meant to be.

o

YOUR WINGS ARE BUILT BY YOUR OWN HANDS.
CREATED FROM THIS DESIRE TO RISE ABOVE THE
CHAOS OF FALLING FOR THE WRONG PERSON.
MAY YOU CONTINUE TO ASCEND IN THE FACES
OF THOSE WHO INTEND TO HURT YOUR HEART.

O

Flames can't hurt the phoenix. She was built from a fire that would scare most people. She was forged in a fire that could never contain her.

o

TAKE A MOMENT TO BREATHE IN COURAGE
SO THAT YOU CAN EXHALE DOUBT.

o

Your worth is not something you'll ever need to negotiate with someone. Your peace is not something you'll ever need to negotiate with someone.

Your existence, your presence, your value. These things are based in and defined by only you.

o

YOU COME TO THIS UNDERSTANDING THAT
YOU ARE NOT LOST; YOU'RE JUST EVOLVING.
YOU ARE IN AN ERA OF REDISCOVERY
AND FINDING MORE OF WHO YOU ARE
AND MORE OF WHAT'S BEEN HIDDEN.

o

THE WINDS OF CHANGE COME FROM
YOUR BREATH; YOU ARE THE STORM.

o

FROM THE ASHES, YOU ARE REBORN. FROM THE
FIRE, THE BIRTH OF A SOUL THAT REFUSES TO BE
CONQUERED, MANIPULATED, OR DIMINISHED.

o

Love can be secure without being tamed. Embrace your wild heart. Embrace an uncaged love.

o

PAIN CAN HELP YOU SHAPE YOURSELF,
BUT IT WILL NEVER DEFINE YOU.

O

THESE SCARS ARE REMINDERS.
THEY ARE NOT CHAINS.

o

FEAR NOT THE RAIN. TODAY'S STORM
IS TOMORROW'S GARDEN.

o

MAY YOU BE WATERED BY YOUR TEARS.

o

EVERYTHING CHANGES WHEN YOU
PRIORITIZE PEACE OVER APPROVAL.

o

Slowly but surely, you are becoming
the person you've always needed.

o

BE FIERCE IN YOUR KINDNESS.

O

You radiate love despite the chaos,
and that alone makes you brilliant.

o

THERE IS A RHYTHM UNFOLDING IN YOUR
JOURNEY. TRUST IT. LET IT LEAD YOU.

o

LOVE IS A GUIDE, AND IT SHOULD
NEVER BE BLINDING.

o

It's a courageous thing, you know?
To love with depth absent of fear,
especially after you've been hurt.

o

LONELINESS CAN OFTEN BE A NURTURER
OF GROWTH AND SELF-LOVE.

O

HERE'S THE TRUTH: YOU AREN'T BROKEN.
YOU'RE JUST TRANSFORMING.

o

Sometimes you have to dance with your demons to show them that they'll never be able to move as fluidly as you.

O

THERE ARE TIMES WHEN YOU'VE FELT
WEAK. TIMES WHEN YOU BELIEVED
YOU'D LOST YOURSELF. BUT RIGHT NOW,
YOU ARE RECLAIMING YOUR STORY AND
WRITING A NEW AND BEAUTIFUL NARRATIVE
OF WHAT IT MEANS TO BE YOU.

○

The universe is writing a poem
with ink made from you.

o

POETRY

she just stood like a mountain
unwavering beneath any storm
her presence, a gentle strength
grounded in peace

O

her heart, like a river
overflowing with love
carving beautiful paths
through stone
intentional and gentle

o

in her mind's eye
the stars, guiding lost souls
a beautiful beacon of light
in the darkest of nights

O

her soul, an oak tree
rooted deep into the earth
held by Mother Nature
branches reaching for the sky
a shelter for those
she's allowed into her life

o

her presence, a whisper
soft as the morning air
powerful enough
to move mountains

o

she emerged as gold
from a fire
a phoenix reborn
with the power
to shift the universe

o

oceans, in her silence
vast, beautiful, and deep
a calm where infinite strength resides

o

she brought a sort of dawn
everywhere she went
breaking the night's hold
promising light
for those weighed down
by the darkness

o

she's in bloom and unbothered
out of reach and at peace in darkness

o

her hand, like the wind
invisible but felt
she brought change
and peace
to everything she touched

o

she, like the rain
gentle and unrelenting
she nourishes and nurtures
with a quiet and elegant persistence

o

her mind
a deep forest of ideas
a sanctuary of peace
a keeper of wisdom

o

she, a child of the moon
reflecting hidden light
a silent guardian
in a midnight sky

O

she burned with passion
unfaltering and brilliant
an eternal light
her spirit a beautiful flame

o

do you notice
the way your heart
feels the weight of confusion
whenever they're near
or how your mind
becomes a prison
a nightmarish home
as you reach for their hand
let go of what pushes you
into an emotional oblivion
hold on to your peace
by moving on

O

there is a gentle awakening
waiting for your heart
there is a newfound freedom
awaiting your presence
despite the chaos you've known
there is beauty waiting for you there
a place where hearts go
when they've decided to heal
and there will always be room for you
when you're ready

o

I remember me
the me before you
before this, before us
I remember me
the joy in the silence
before you ever spoke
the time I spent alone
before embracing your presence
I remember me
the one who knows
how to live without you

o

she is an endless spring
in every season
from her soul's soil
new blossoms of self grow
with the scent of brilliance

o

love her hard
and she'll be soft
with you

o

my dream of love
was the only reason
I survived this nightmare
my sense of longing
was the only thing
that kept me reaching
for everything you were not
I think it was the hate in your eyes
that helped me realize
that the love I needed
was elsewhere
or your inconsiderate nature
that pushed me to a tribe of people
who genuinely consider
the way I feel
thank you for hurting me
in doing so
I discovered healing
I discovered an exit

o

you, a force of nature
your presence awakens
cherry blossoms in spring

you, a light of great magnitude
the sun is your only rival
you cast yourself into darkness
so that courage can exist

o

starving for healthy attention
eager for something better
you discovered that true love
was an inside job
the moment you decided
to fall for yourself

o

I love the part of me
that refuses
to let you destroy
my ideas of love

I love the part of me
that no longer
withholds the truth
out of fear of being lied on
or lied to

I love the part of me
that forgave everything
you never apologized for

I love that part of me
that values peace
over staying
in an unhealthy relationship

o

built for love
so that when heartache arrives
there's joy on the other side
of what you lost

a peace in knowing
that their absence
is an opportunity
to dive deeper
into the realms of self-love

in their absence lives a chance
to fill that space with someone
more aligned with who you are becoming

be built for love
cultivate it
maintain it on your own
so that love can sustain itself
even when others overlook
all that you are

be built for love
so that when someone leaves
they provide space
for stronger connections

be built for love
in preparation
for what is trying to find you

you see, love is never truly far
from the person who deserves it
love is never too far
for the person who proves to be capable
of giving themselves everything
that no one else has been able to provide

love will always come to you
because you've provided
a safe space for it to thrive
you are built for love

o

she bloomed
through
the broken feelings

o

stop waiting for something
you can already give yourself

o

a calm love is the only love
that can reach her

o

observe her in full appreciation
she is the essence of summer

o

light workers need lovers
who amplify and cherish
their inner peace and ability to heal

o

she wasn't waiting for you
she gave herself a soft life

o

before you love the flower
appreciate her roots

o

a narcissist's apology
is just a lie

o

in the dim glow of candlelight, your eyes
two beautiful pools of mystic gold
a spiced and delicious surprise
silky whispers in the shadows as you move
every gesture your body makes
a poem, each line fiery and brilliant
your laughter, soft, a melody of the night
it dances through the air
the distance between us begins to blur
the heat of any idea of you
a tender murmur in my brain
touch traced like art upon your skin
with my fingers in a fantasy
our souls are so close
to the discovery of love
I'm eager to find you

o

LOVE LETTERS
TO THE UNIVERSE
INSIDE YOU

.

I can be eager for you at times. My sense of longing reaches its highest levels when my heart is in a good mood. There's a beautiful, calming energy floating inside me. It's in those moments where I wonder if you'd consider having me, taking me in, sharing in whatever I'm willing to give unto you.

I think we love differently each time, especially when the love given is wholly matched. It takes on a different form, tells a different story, and holds a different meaning. We become something entirely different over time as well. The wounds from where we've loved and been taken for granted eventually heal, and we transform and come out the other end with newfound respect and acknowledgment for what our hearts truly need.

This is why I'm always okay with an ending. The end is necessary to bring forth the type of love that isn't toxic. The type of love that can withstand time. The type of love that doesn't put the heart in danger.

See, we think alike. We're after the same thing.

o

Just like the sun's fire, a woman's strength blazes brightly, warming the hearts of those around her and illuminating the path forward.

Her strength is like the moon's light: soft yet resilient, guiding us through the darkest hours of the night with gentle clarity.

A woman's strength radiates with the intensity of the sun, burning away anything that no longer serves her.

Her strength is a quiet beacon in the dark, like the moon, promising hope and direction amid uncertainty.

Even in the darkest nights, her strength reveals beauty in the struggle, teaching us the power of a woman who knows what her heart deserves.

o

Isn't it beautiful? The complete understanding that, even if you aren't where you want to be, all it takes is mindset and physical action to move your life into the most beautiful era it has ever experienced.

I know it's never easy—you see, a life of peace and joy often requires an uphill battle filled with plenty of obstacles—but you have to remember that when faced with the choice to quit or keep going, you have always decided to power through the madness. That's why you're here right now, reading these words.

I'm right there with you, fighting for a greater capacity for love. Longing for extended moments of bliss. Actively sustaining peace even when external forces make a play at destroying it. I'm in the mud with you, feeling this overwhelming need to be cleansed. I know it's been a long fight, but there's only a little bit further to go. Hold on.

It's important to give yourself grace. It's important to take a moment to acknowledge how far you've come in your journey. It gets weary, holding it all in while trying to hold it together on your own. Not only that, but there have been people in your life who have either hurt you or held you back from reaching your destination. But it's never too late to take back your power, your time, and your energy.

Love you; take care.

o

It appears impossible, that idea that someone embodies characteristics that feel like they're tailor-made for you and your life. It's a rare sighting, like an eclipse, the sun meeting the face of the moon, or a river sitting in the center of a desert. You move through life, facing obstacles in the form of people who are playing their part in distracting you from finding your person, and some of them believe they are that person, even as they seem to be deliberately fracturing your heart. You try your best to navigate these spaces of disappointment and possible regret. You struggle with that so much and for so long that you nearly give up on the thought of finding your match, so much so that you even settle and pretend that the person you're with was meant for you. But the moment your head hits the pillow, you lie there wide-awake, trying to piece together the set of events that made you even think you could stay or that it could last.

It appears impossible, but it isn't. You feel it as you read this, don't you? Those senses of longing, these words remind you that there is something greater than what you've known, and there is someone out there willing to be more than the person you've settled for. You lose yourself when you give in to this idea that true love isn't real or that soulmates don't exist, and you've lost yourself time and time again, but as your eyes dance over this page, consuming my every word, you're starting to believe again, and your belief in love will help preserve your heart for the one who deserves you.

Never allow yourself to be so torn down by people who don't love you that you forget that the one who always will is out there searching and preparing themselves to be with someone like you.

For all the moments of love you've given, for all the devotion and effort you've invested, there is someone out there in the world who will never make you feel like your best isn't enough.

We're all on this beautiful journey toward love together. And I'm living for the moment when love finally meets you in the heart.

○

I was staring at the moon the other night, full of light, giving life to my belief in your existence. I marvel at the stars for a moment, and then my mind wanders off and questions how bright you shine. Is your heart full like the moon outside my window? Is its weight all inspired by joy or pain? Have you been smiling through the heartache, or have you kept yourself hidden so that no one could know?

I stare out into the night, catching glimpses of you moving through the sky like a wind that is eager to embrace a lover. I open the window with this hope that I am what you've been reaching for. And somewhere in your journey, you may find yourself here, sharing this moment with me. I, the writer, and you, the inspiration for every word written on this page.

o

You're the most beautiful soul I can think of . . . someone who, despite having their heart broken several times, shows up in this moment with the idea of true love still intact. I find myself being inspired by your essence every single day. While there are moments when you feel invisible or ignored, sometimes overlooked and unappreciated, magic dwells within you, more significant than anything in this world. I'd like you to know that the love you think about, the love you long for, the love that is waiting for you at the end of this storm, is the most beautiful love you'll ever experience in your entire life, and I am grateful for the opportunity to be the one to remind you.

o

There's so much that I want to tell you, and even as I write these words, I'm afraid that the sentiment here will fail to express this profound desire to meet you in the middle of love.

There are moments in the day when time begins to move so slowly, it feels like my feelings for you have become nearly frozen in time. I gaze inward as if looking into a mirror, searching for you in my heart's most peaceful rooms. You move through me like an idea eager to exist in the external world, and a part of me wishes that the words living here on this page will be read by you and that somehow you'll know how I really feel.

o

I can hear our laughter somewhere out in the distance, your soft lips gently coming together to repeat the thing that made us laugh, the warmth of your touch as you reach for me in that moment of bliss. I hear and see it all so vividly. So when they ask me how I know true love exists, I tell them it is because of you and how you appear in my dreams as everything I've always wanted.

You sneak up on me like a wonderful surprise; it's like you always seem to know when I need it most, the thoughtfulness in the idea of being loved by you, the security in knowing that I could be yours. Not once in my life has anyone wanted to treat me kindly, or, at least, not in the long-term sense. They come and go, usually souring in the end or whenever they're finished using me as a source for whatever it is they need at the time. But I'm no victim, and as strange as it may sound, I'll happily be discarded if that means being found by you.

I believe in a once-in-a-lifetime love, a partner who doesn't need to make a relationship difficult. Someone who understands what it means to be happy because they have taken on the responsibility of cultivating those feelings within themselves, and in doing so, they've sustained a level of accountability that is often rare in today's relationships. A lifetime of love with a partner who values peace just as much as I do. Someone who, in their daily practice, maintains a frame of mind that creates a beautiful picture of life. Someone who makes decisions for the greater good, absent of selfishness and ego. Someone like you, the one reading these words right now.

So, when they ask me how I know true love exists, I close my eyes and point to you.

o

MY INTENTION IS NOT TO SAVE YOU.
I ONLY WANT TO BE CLOSE ENOUGH
TO WITNESS A WOMAN BECOME MORE
BRILLIANT THAN SHE'S EVER BEEN.

O

Sometimes, you feel a sort of rain in your chest. You're sweet, and your kind nature makes the heartache almost look beautiful as it happens to you. You feel sadness, but you nearly smile through it. There is a wealth of chaos occurring in your mind, and yet you're always there for everyone. You're strong, of course, but sometimes you get tired of pretending that these storms are not tearing you down. Nevertheless, you continue to fight and push forward, putting less and less distance between yourself and the things you want to feel, and this is what makes you brilliant.

And I guess this is why I find myself writing about you all the time. You find these words and realize they're meant for you. Listen, the journey that stretches into what you deserve is a tough one, and this, for you, is just a reminder. A mirror, perhaps. I hope you find these words whenever you forget who you are.

o

Years of mistrust and disappointment . . .
I wonder what that has done to you in your pursuit of a love that I've been eager to give. There are these moments when the thought of you and everything you've struggled with shows up in my daily meditations. And so, I find myself pausing amid that stillness to give you room to dwell inside me.

You're mighty in the way you exist. There is a magic that resides inside your soul, and you find new and beautiful ways to shine your light whenever the hours are dark. I sometimes find myself searching for you in those darker shades of blue, when sadness finds me and I'm unable to get out of whatever hole I've fallen into.

The idea of you is heaven; the thought of you is like a tropical oasis whenever gray skies hover above my head. I find you in a dream, and the nightmares cease.

I believe we are possibly kindred in both the pain we've experienced and the healing work we've been doing for ourselves in an effort to free our hearts of everything that no longer serves us or the future. And this is why you more than likely feel that I'm speaking to you, because I am.

Our journeys, filled with both challenges and opportunities for growth and deep connections, are underpinned by a resilience born of our struggles, drawing us closer despite distance and obstacles. By believing in the universe's power to align souls of similar frequencies—those of love, understanding, and respect—we share a connection that transcends solitude and is celebrated under the stars, embodying the true essence of love as a safe haven. As I envision our paths merging into a future free from mistrust and disappointment, basking in shared experiences, I stand ready to embark on this adventure with you, embracing the love that defines our purpose, joy, and peace. In the subtle signs of nature, I sense your presence, fueling my belief in our potential unity. I invite you to join me in this leap toward a new beginning, where, hand in hand, we'll explore the boundless possibilities of love and freedom.

○

LAST NIGHT, I CALLED ON THE NIGHT SKY TO
SHARE A STORY ABOUT YOU. I KNOW THE MOON
HAS SOMETIMES BEEN THE MOST CONSISTENT
THING IN YOUR LIFE, AND IT HAS WITNESSED
SO MUCH OF WHAT IS KEPT HIDDEN INSIDE
YOUR HEART. THE MOON HAS SINCE KNOWN
THINGS THAT ARE JUST NOW DRIFTING TO ME
WHENEVER I'M IN SOLITUDE, IN THE PRACTICE
OF MINDFULNESS. BUT I WAS EAGER FOR AN
ANSWER, EAGER FOR THE OPPORTUNITY TO
FEEL CLOSER TO YOU AT THAT MOMENT. SO
I CLOSED MY EYES UPON THE MOON'S REQUEST,
AND IT WAS YOUR VOICE THAT I BEGAN TO HEAR,
NEARLY SPATIAL IN ITS DYNAMIC. I COULD
FEEL YOU LIKE A WHISPER IN BOTH EARS.

O

There's a look of love in your eyes as you read this. A love that's been through trails of fire, a love that has been overlooked, sometimes deemed not good enough by those who were incapable of truly seeing the magic in your heart. Consider the idea that as you read this, it's reading you. Seeing you for all that you are, becoming a mirror, catching the light on your face and in your soul, and then bouncing it back to you in an effort to make you smile.

It's easy for me to speak to you in a tone that feels familiar because I know exactly where you are. I've sat in that same place, nursing my wounds while trying my hardest not to lose sight of a love better than anything I've had. Knowing that if I stopped believing in true love, I'd be compromising the opportunity to be with someone like you in the future.

o

THE ROOTS OF A GOOD WOMAN ARE AN INFINITE
BRIDGE INTO A BEAUTIFUL UNKNOWN. SHE
LIVES AND BLOOMS FROM THE RICHEST SOIL;
EXPANDING AND MOVING IN THE WINDS OF
HER OWN INTENTION; SURVIVING OFF LAND
NURTURED BY HER OWN SPIRIT, THIS EARTH,
THIS PLANET; SITTING IN THE UNIVERSE THAT
SHE IMAGINED. A DREAM TRANSFORMED INTO
A TANGIBLE THING. A VISION THAT MOST WILL
FIND DIFFICULT TO COMPREHEND, AND STILL SHE
EXISTS. UNAFRAID OF BEING MISUNDERSTOOD,
OVERLOOKED, AND UNAPPRECIATED. SHE HAS
FEARS, BUT SHE REFUSES TO ALLOW THOSE
OBSTACLES TO STOP HER, BECAUSE EVERYTHING
IN HER WAY INSPIRES HER TO BE MORE THAN
ANYTHING THEY THOUGHT SHE COULD BE, AND
THAT ALONE MAKES HER THE MOST BEAUTIFUL
THING IN EXISTENCE. THAT ALONE MAKES
HER THE MOST BEAUTIFUL PERSON TO ME.

O

I have this reoccurring dream of us, you, standing in Drottningholm Palace Park, the wind playing in your hair. Your eyes on fire, filled with summer and love. Me, armed with a camera to capture a dream within a dream. Your lips move to produce a whisper, holding the warmth of everything I need to hear. You stare into me like you've found your home, and as I begin to step toward you, I wake up. The time is always 3:33.

o

I LONG TO KNOW YOU, MY HANDS WARM WITH A
FEVER, EAGER TO FEEL YOUR FINGERTIPS. MY
TONGUE A RESTING PLACE FOR YOUR NAME, MY
LIPS MADE TO LIE UPON YOURS. IF THE MOON
COULD TALK, IT WOULD SPEAK OF MY LOVE AND
ADMIRATION FOR YOUR EXISTENCE. THE WAY
YOU MOVE THROUGH TIME WITH GRACE, THE
WAY YOU STAND FIRM IN YOUR BELIEF OF LOVE.
THE WAY YOU REFUSE TO SETTLE WHERE MAGIC
ISN'T PROVIDED TO MATCH THE MAGIC WITHIN
YOU. WITH A BULLETPROOF SOUL, YOU'VE
MANAGED TO REACH ME, AND IN THIS MOMENT,
I WANT NOTHING MORE THAN TO REACH BACK.

o

To be continued . . .

EPILOGUE

The phases of the moon provide a beautiful metaphor for the healing journey, as both involve cycles of growth, change, and renewal. What follows is a comparison of the moon's phases to the stages of a healing journey.

A new moon is representative of the start of the healing process. This is a time for introspection, observation, and figuring out which areas of your life are in need of healing. This is a time to set intentions for personal growth and recovery.

A waxing crescent focuses on the initial activation and the steps taken toward healing. There is a profound sense of hope and potential in forward progress as you begin to implement changes that will assist you in cultivating healthier habits.

In the first quarter, half the moon is illuminated, which can symbolize challenges in decision-making. This phase is representative of facing obstacles and making important decisions in the process of healing. This phase often requires an abundance of courage and determination to continue forward in hopes of making progress despite all the difficulties.

During the waxing gibbous, you enter a space in which you get to practice and fine-tune your efforts. In this moment, you reflect on what has been working and what will need to be adjusted. This is a time for deep preparation and persistence as you approach major breakthroughs.

The full moon in all its glory represents a peak in your healing journey. This is a time set for many realizations, understanding, and emotional release. The full moon brings with it plenty of clarity and the results of all your efforts, often leading to a deeper, more profound level of self-awareness.

Waning gibbous is a time to express gratitude for the progress you've made along your journey. It's a moment to look over the data, maybe share your insights, and seek some support from the ones you love. This is a time when you apply your greatest level of nurturing the seeds of your present to look forward to a future that is filled with peace and love due to all the work you've done.

The last quarter involves the work of letting go of what no longer serves you. It is a time to shed old patterns, beliefs, and emotions that hinder further progress. Embrace this process of removal, for it is one of the most essential acts in changing the direction of your life and making room for the right things to hold space in your life.

The waning crescent is the final phase of the healing cycle, and it reflects a period of rest and renewal. This is a moment to integrate the lessons you've learned and prepare for the next cycle of growth and healing. In this stage, you must always emphasize the importance of self-care and rejuvenation.

Your journey toward healing is just like the moon and its phases, and I hope the words here have helped you along the way. In my own journey to this phase in my life, I've found solace in daily reflections and centering my heart in the space of love, which has given me the inspiration to write all this to you. As we look toward the new chapters, I just want to take the time to express my love and admiration for the person who decided to pick up this book. Thank you for remaining strong and maintaining this belief in yourself that has carried you through some of the darkest phases of your life. While this book has come to an end, the work we are doing on ourselves and together still continues. I'm hoping we'll meet again.

New Moons copyright © 2025 by r.h. Sin. All rights reserved.
Printed in the United States of America. No part of this book may
be used or reproduced in any manner whatsoever without written
permission, except in the case of reprints in the context of reviews.

Andrews McMeel Publishing
a division of Andrews McMeel Universal
1130 Walnut Street, Kansas City, Missouri 64106

www.andrewsmcmeel.com

25 26 27 28 29 LAK 10 9 8 7 6 5 4 3 2 1

ISBN: 979-8-8816-0017-4

Library of Congress Control Number: 2024941597

Editor: Patty Rice
Art Director: Diane Marsh
Production Editor: Kayla Overbey
Production Manager: Shona Burns

ATTENTION: SCHOOLS AND BUSINESSES
Andrews McMeel books are available at quantity discounts
with bulk purchase for educational, business, or sales
promotional use. For information, please email the Andrews
McMeel Publishing Special Sales Department:
sales@andrewsmcmeel.com.